This Was Meant To Find You

When You Needed It Most

CHARLOTTE FREEMAN

THOUGHT
CATALOG
Books

THOUGHTCATALOG.COM

THOUGHT CATALOG Books

Published by Thought Catalog Books, an imprint of Thought Catalog, a digital magazine owned and operated by The Thought & Expression Co. Inc., an independent media organization founded in 2010 and based in the United States of America. For stocking inquiries, contact stockists@shopcatalog.com.

Produced by Chris Lavergne and Noelle Beams
Art direction and design by KJ Parish
Circulation management by Isidoros Karamitopoulos

thoughtcatalog.com | shopcatalog.com

First Edition, Limited Edition Pressing
Printed in the United States of America

ISBN 978-1-949759-64-8

at all. This was meant to find you on the days that you're struggling to see your worth and find yourself believing in everyone but yourself. This was meant to find you when you're feeling confused or lost entirely. This was meant to find you in your deepest moments of vulnerability. This was meant to find you in your journey of finding yourself, your journey of healing. This was meant to find you in your moments of pure joy and genuine happiness. This was meant to find you if you are still looking for that.

This was meant to find you *when you needed it most.*

CHASER

You should never regret going after what makes your heart happy, even if it has ended in hurt. Instead, you should feel so beyond proud of yourself for being brave enough to chase what makes you feel alive. There are some people out there who are too afraid to chase their dreams who admire that strength in you. You should always feel proud of yourself for knowing what you want and taking steps to obtain it. So I hope you never regret anything that becomes such an important part of your journey, of finding happiness, and discovering who you are as a person.

GROWING THROUGH IT

I hope you are learning to give yourself the credit you deserve. I hope you are beginning to recognize just how strong you are for pulling yourself through each and every difficult time in your life. I hope you allow this realization to walk with you, alongside any obstacles or roadblocks you might encounter along your journey. I hope you know just how capable you are and that no matter how challenging a situation may seem, you have the courage to keep moving, to keep growing, and to keep healing. I hope you can look in the mirror and say, '*I'm proud of you*' and really mean it. And above all, I hope you realize just how incredible you are, and just how much you deserve your own love.

No one can get you to
where you want to be
but you.

MAGICAL HORIZONS

Sometimes you lose a love to find a love that's deeper, kinder, stronger. Sometimes you lose an opportunity because there is something even more magical on the horizon. Sometimes you lose a friend because you've outgrown each other and are holding one another back. Sometimes you lose yourself because you're about to discover a more profound reason for living, an undeniable purpose which defines your true path.

Remember this when you feel like something is slipping away from you before you are ready to let go: the opportunities and people you lose along the way are the stepping-stones paving your way to your happiest self, your truest love, your most genuine purpose. What's waiting for you on the other side of this pain and uncertainty will be worth all the stones in your path; and I promise you won't want to change a thing about your journey once you see where it's taking you.

SELFISH LOVER

Why is it that the ones who hurt us only try to come back once we learn to live without them? I often wonder what goes through the mind of someone who tears the soul out of another only to see if they can grab it once more, knowing they don't want to hold it for anyone else's benefit but their own. I often wonder how someone can demand your love back because it makes them feel validated, yet have no intention of loving you in the right way, or in some cases, *loving you at all.* This selfish kind of love somehow pulls you back in even after you *know* you are better off without it. This selfish kind of love pulls you back even after you *know* you deserve so much more. This selfish kind of love does not deserve to play tug of war with your heart when you are trying to move on from your pain.

Allow yourself
to sit with your pain
as long as you need to
allow your pain
to teach you
all that it needs to teach
but do not allow it
to define you
because you are such a
beautiful composition
of so much more than
the things that have
broken you.

EXTRAORDINARY

This is just the beginning. You have so much more to do and discover. Even if it feels like you should be further along by now, be patient with yourself; good things take time and there is no need to rush this beautiful journey you are on. Take each day as it comes and make the most of it. Rest easy knowing that things are falling into place, and everything is coming together just like how you hoped they would in your mind. Don't waste any of your precious breaths comparing your progress to anyone else. Inspiration goes so much further than comparison and you're far too special and unique to measure your success by external factors. Good things take time, and my dear, you're destined for the extraordinary.

LOVE NOTES

Be gentle with yourself if it's taking you a little too long to realize that love isn't supposed to be painful, toxic or hard. The people who make you feel like you are hard to love are not worthy of your heart. You deserve to receive the kind of love that makes your heart feel calm, assured, and secure. You deserve to feel the kind of love you have always dreamed about. You deserve the same energy that you give.

SLOW DANCE

It's okay if you're moving slow, or taking a break *entirely*. It's okay to pace yourself and take your time. Sometimes the *only* person putting pressure on a situation is *you*. It's okay to go a little easier on yourself. It's okay to be *human*.

SOMETIMES THERE IS NO REASON

It's comforting to believe that everything happens for a reason *(and sometimes this does prove to be true)* but sometimes heartbreaking things can happen and it seems like there is no possible way to explain the situation, or reason with it—not right now anyway. Situations arise sometimes that simply just do not make sense. You may find yourself asking *"how could something like this happen to someone like me?"* or *"why do bad things happen to good people?"* or *"why wasn't I enough?"* While you may search for a meaning or a reason behind this pain, it's important to remember that sometimes there is no reason, sometimes things don't happen for any reason at all. Maybe you did nothing to deserve this, maybe you won't find a reason this time, maybe you *were* always enough. Sometimes life can be cruel, even to the kindest hearts and the softest souls on this planet. But oh my, life can also be beautiful. So, so beautiful. Please remember that there is always sunshine after the rain, light after the dark. If you can't find a reason for your pain right now—at least have trust that better things are on their way to you, even if it doesn't feel like it. Always know that day by day, little by little, your heart is healing and getting ready to let all the goodness radiate back towards you. Beautiful things are coming, please keep your heart open to them, and above all, please believe that you are worthy of it all.

Life becomes more beautiful
when you begin to choose yourself.

YOU DESERVE IT ALL

Have you ever worked too hard on things that don't make you happy? Or put too much of yourself into the wrong relationships to the point where you're working so hard to make something work for the wrong reasons, because that's what society makes you believe you should do?

There can be so much pressure on finding 'success' or finding the 'perfect person' that you put your happiness aside and keep trying to make something work when all it's doing is chipping away at your soul, your authenticity, and your happiness. It can feel like there is so much pressure to succeed in all aspects of life, that suddenly you completely forget what makes your soul feel alive in order to keep up.

This is your reminder that success comes in so many forms and is different to everyone. Success can also be found by following your heart and putting yourself first. Success can be found by letting go of something you didn't want to let go of but knowing why you had to. Success can be found by making the right choices for yourself even if it doesn't make sense to everyone around you. Success is realizing that you deserve more than what you currently have and being brave enough to make a change.

I hope you are brave enough to find the success you are looking for, even if that means letting go of the things that no longer serve you. And I hope you don't let anyone make you believe that you are giving up on someone or something, when you know deep down that you are making the right choice for yourself and your future.

—You deserve to live a life that makes *you* happy.

LITTLE PIECES

I know that your heart has been shattered into a million little pieces at the hands of others and how afraid that makes you feel to fall deeply for someone again. I know how vulnerable that makes your heart feel and the anxiety that comes along with that. I know that it's easier to put your walls back up and block love out because it's the most reliable way to ensure your heart won't ever be at risk of being so badly broken again. I know that's the easiest way because I have been there too.

But I promise you this one thing, nothing grows in that state, nothing grows when you close yourself off to the opportunity of loving again. And this is because when you close your heart you are also closing down on yourself, you are closing down on who you really are, you are letting yourself slip further and further away from your true self and what makes you feel like you. I know you love to love, so why are you taking that away from yourself? I promise you that not everybody you encounter is going to grab your heart so disrespectfully, I promise you that there *are* people out there who will take your heart so lovingly, and count their blessings each day that they have the chance to hold it.

I promise you that there are people out there who will understand the language of your heart and what you have been through and they will show you so much patience and understanding while you heal. I promise you that your feelings, your anxiety, and your trauma are not a burden to the ones who love you and I promise you that you are capable of giving and receiving love *despite it all*.

I wish you could see just how worthy you are of good things, of genuine love, of deep connections, of happiness. I wish you could escape your mind for just one moment and see everything you deserve, because once you see it, once you feel it, you can't deny that it's real. You are worth so much more than the way you've been made to feel in the past, and your past experiences do not define your future or your ability to be loved the right way, to be loved at all. I hope you find it in yourself to open up your heart again, just a little more each day, and let a little bit of love back in. I hope that in doing so you begin to see all the things that are meant for you finding their way to you, and I hope you acknowledge that you are worthy of it all.

It's okay to feel whatever you're feeling right now.
It's okay to feel whatever you're feeling right now.
It's okay to feel whatever you're feeling right now.
It's okay to feel whatever you're feeling right now.
It's okay to feel whatever you're feeling right now.
It's okay to feel whatever you're feeling right now.
It's okay to feel whatever you're feeling right now.
It's okay to feel whatever you're feeling right now.
It's okay to feel whatever you're feeling right now.
It's okay to feel whatever you're feeling right now.
It's okay to feel whatever you're feeling right now.
It's okay to feel whatever you're feeling right now.
It's okay to feel whatever you're feeling right now.
It's okay to feel whatever you're feeling right now.
It's okay to feel whatever you're feeling right now.
It's okay to feel whatever you're feeling right now.
It's okay to feel whatever you're feeling right now.
It's okay to feel whatever you're feeling right now.
It's okay to feel whatever you're feeling right now.
It's okay to feel whatever you're feeling right now.
It's okay to feel whatever you're feeling right now.
It's okay to feel whatever you're feeling right now.
It's okay to feel whatever you're feeling right now.
It's okay to feel whatever you're feeling right now.
It's okay to feel whatever you're feeling right now.
It's okay to feel whatever you're feeling right now.
It's okay to feel whatever you're feeling right now.

DAYS LIKE THESE

There will be days where the simple tasks don't feel so simple. Days where you know you could have achieved it all if your mind wasn't so tired. Days where you try to get yourself into the mindset you know you *can* get into but for some reason today it just isn't happening. Days where all of a sudden time has run out and instead of giving your body the break it needed you wasted a whole day pushing yourself to get through it but didn't achieve anything at all. These are the days where you're too burnt out to give it everything it needs, but for some reason you still try, maybe because you're afraid of letting someone down, or letting yourself down. Why is there so much stigma around taking a day off when your mind doesn't feel so good? For some reason, or maybe even no reason at all, you just can't do it today, and that's okay. Take the time you need to rest, to find inspiration, to remember all the little things that make you happy. It's those little things that help remind you who you are, and why you do what you do. Your mind wasn't created to be 'on' like this all the time, constantly rushed and pushed beyond its limits, day after day. Normalize accepting this and stop forcing yourself to "just get through it" when you know deep down your mind needs a break. Look after yourself, look after your mind, and see what magic you're capable of.

—*Burnout*

Never forget that you deserve
what your heart desires.

Never forget that you are capable
of what your heart desires.

YOU ARE ENOUGH

You are enough even when you don't feel like it. Even on your darkest days, you know, the ones when you don't even feel like getting out of bed, you're enough on those days too. You are enough even when your heart has been hurt by someone you love and care about. You know those days when you stand in front of the mirror and don't feel like yourself, you're enough on those days too. When you're exhausted, run off your feet and didn't finish everything you needed to that day, you're enough then too. You are enough. You always are and you always have been. Be kind to yourself. Today and always.

YOU COME FIRST

It's great to look after others, but don't forget to look after yourself too. It's lovely that you help people achieve their goals, but don't forget that your hopes and dreams are worthy of coming true too. You're allowed to say no if something doesn't serve you. You're allowed to say no if something doesn't feel right. Don't betray yourself for the sake of someone else's happiness. Learn to recognize when this is happening because that's likely when you need to say no or put some boundaries in place to protect yourself. It's not selfish to make yourself the most important person in your life. It's important to be there for others, but don't forget to be there for yourself too.

—*Reminders for those who always put other people first.*

Sometimes *all it takes*
for you to do it
is to *finally* decide
how much you want it.

THINGS TO LET GO OF

Too often we hold onto things that are damaging us and we fail to see just how much we deserve, because it's the easiest thing to believe when we are doubting ourselves. The truth is, we are all a lot happier when we finally begin to let go of whatever is dragging us down.

Let go of one-sided relationships. Let go of the people whose actions do not match their words. These relationships pull you down and don't contribute to your growth. Be brave enough to put yourself first and finally let them go. It's hard at first but what follows is so worth it and once you experience that feeling you will agree.

Let go of the guilt you feel for not doing it all at once. Be proud of yourself just for making it this far. There is still so much time to make magic happen.

Let go of the fear of failure. Let go of the idea that it's too late to succeed. You have everything you need to succeed already within you. Release your self-doubt and go after everything you know you can achieve. Do not tempt yourself into staying in the same place forever, just because it's comfortable.

Let go of competitive energy. Stop comparing yourself to those around you and try to see your own true worth. There is space for you to be everything you dream to be, and once you focus on yourself instead of those around you, it becomes so much easier to achieve your goals without all the unnecessary, outside noise.

Let go of your limiting beliefs. They are more damaging than you think. The way you speak to yourself matters and if your mind gets used to a negative narrative, your mind will have a negative outlook.

If you are feeling stuck, think about everything that you are holding onto. Let go of anything that is making your soul feel heavy, let go of anything that is making your heart feel burnt out and your mind feel tired, let go of anything that is making you feel like you do not deserve more. Please believe that you deserve to feel free of all the things you're carrying that were never actually yours to hold onto. Because you deserve to breathe without burden and feel happiness without the fear of someone taking it away from you once more.

LIGHTEN THE LOAD

I hope you know that you don't have to carry the weight of the world on your *own*. I hope you know that there are people out there who are happy to share the load. I hope you know that your past does not define you, and that it's okay to let go of it, little by little, day by day, until the weight of what you're carrying doesn't make you feel like you're stuck, unable to move in the direction you're longing to move in, unable to move *at all*. I hope you allow yourself to heal, because you deserve to walk through this life with a purpose. I hope you know that it's okay to release your grip and begin to set yourself free.

LET'S FALL IN LOVE

Let's fall in love with making each day more beautiful than the last. Let's fall in love with ourselves a little more each day and with every messy and uncomfortable thing we learn about ourselves while doing so. Let's fall in love with making mistakes in order to grow. Let's fall in love with taking risks and taking meaningful steps outside our comfort zones. Let's fall in love with the littlest things in life, the biggest things, and absolutely everything in-between. Let's fall in love with prioritizing ourselves and the way that looking after our minds and bodies makes us feel. Let's fall in love with life and everything on this planet that makes you feel like you belong here. Let's fall in love with chasing happiness and each moment that helps you catch it. Let's open our hearts and let love in—in every way imaginable. Let's fall in love with the gift we have been given to be right here, right now. Let's fall in love with each other and watch the beauty bloom from our soft hearts and shine light onto the world.

SEASONS

This is for anybody going through a tough season right now. Please be gentle with yourself. When the world seems dark it's only fair that you are compassionate with yourself while you navigate your way at this time. We are all doing the best we know how to at the moment and you are no different. I want you to know that you're not alone. I promise you that whatever you are feeling, there is someone else feeling it all with you. I encourage you to reach out to someone and share what you're feeling, you'll learn so quickly how much support you have around you, and you're not as isolated as you feel.

Please remember that nothing is permanent. This season will pass. On the other side of this pain and uncertainty is strength, happiness, and growth. Focus on this feeling, focus on how proud of yourself you will be once you pull yourself through this season and into the next. You have pulled yourself through every hard time so far and you'll pull yourself through this too. Be kind to yourself, be patient with yourself, and be honest with your feelings. Become comfortable sharing your feelings when they start to over- whelm you. It's truly amazing how clear your mind can feel once you get everything out of your head—it almost gives you an instant sense of clarity and calm.

MOVE MOUNTAINS

You were not put on this earth to stay in the same place forever, you were put on this earth to move mountains and make magic. I know you know this already; you're just having trouble finding the motivation to finally change, to grow and take action. Whenever you are feeling lost or held back by your self-limiting beliefs, try to remember what it is you're after, remember what it is that makes your soul sing and feel like you have a purpose. I know it's hard to find the motivation you need when you're unsure on what you are working towards, which is why first you need to find clarity on *what* you're working towards. Remember that there will be days where you might still struggle to find motivation, but you can't let that set you back. Tomorrow is a new day, and you are doing your best. Keep going, keep growing.

You will never be a burden to the ones who love you.
You will never be a burden to the ones who love you.
You will never be a burden to the ones who love you.
You will never be a burden to the ones who love you.
You will never be a burden to the ones who love you.
You will never be a burden to the ones who love you.
You will never be a burden to the ones who love you.
You will never be a burden to the ones who love you.
You will never be a burden to the ones who love you.
You will never be a burden to the ones who love you.
You will never be a burden to the ones who love you.
You will never be a burden to the ones who love you.
You will never be a burden to the ones who love you.
You will never be a burden to the ones who love you.
You will never be a burden to the ones who love you.
You will never be a burden to the ones who love you.
You will never be a burden to the ones who love you.
You will never be a burden to the ones who love you.
You will never be a burden to the ones who love you.
You will never be a burden to the ones who love you.
You will never be a burden to the ones who love you.
You will never be a burden to the ones who love you.
You will never be a burden to the ones who love you.
You will never be a burden to the ones who love you.
You will never be a burden to the ones who love you.
You will never be a burden to the ones who love you.

THE RIGHT ONE

Let the wrong kind of person show you all the ways that you deserve to be loved by the *right one*. Let the pain of the past be a lesson for *what's to come*. Wait for a love that feels exactly as you always thought it would, wait for a love that feels like something you haven't felt before. Wait for a love that is calm, a love that doesn't consume you, but encourages you to grow. Wait for a love that doesn't make you question yourself or your future. Wait for a love that holds your heart gently, because you deserve the softest kind of love.

—Because what a beautiful moment it is when you realize that your heart is capable of healing again even after it has been broken.

MOVING FORWARD

Moving forward is one of the hardest challenges we are faced with but it can also be the most rewarding. Letting go of something that is no longer serving you is the ultimate freedom; it is the ultimate act of self-care. Especially when after so much time you realize that the head and the heart won't ever come to an agreement. Letting go is heart-breaking. There are some things that do make it easier though, and it's all about trusting yourself and trusting your decision.

If you start to question yourself, you need to remember exactly what you were feeling when you started to think about why it might be time to move forward. Do you have doubts, are you questioning yourself more than you used to? Have you lost your sense of self? At some point this situation became something you no longer wanted and you are honoring yourself by making a decision that will better your life. You've done the hard part by facing this realization, don't let yourself down now because you're afraid of the unknown, because you're afraid to leave your comfort zone.

I know that the mind can wander to places that you don't want to go to, but over-analyzing the past is not productive. You can't go back in time, you can only go forwards. Try to encourage your thoughts to follow this ethos too. Trust that your new path will bring you everything you need to be happy. The past is in the past for a reason. If something was absolutely meant for you, it wouldn't now be in your past and you wouldn't be questioning it, you'd just know. Trust that. Think forwards, move forwards, always.

Remember that your mind sometimes has the power to play tricks on you. Don't succumb to these thoughts. Sometimes, on days when you are feeling low or doubting yourself, your mind can wander and make you question why you even wanted to move on in the first place. Missing someone can make you ask yourself these questions too. Do not give in to these emotions. Be gentle with yourself, rest your mind and remember that tomorrow is a new day and I promise it will bring more clarity than you have right now. Don't let one moment of doubt hold *so much* power over *so much* certainty, over all the work you have done on yourself, over what you know deep down is true.

ONE SMALL THOUGHT

Everything begins from one small thought. Stop doubting yourself and believing in things that are holding you back. Your thoughts hold so much power, both the negative and the positive. Become more aware of your limiting beliefs, have they served you in the past? Challenge yourself to put more focus on the positive ones and watch how the way you think about yourself changes. Remember that all the best ideas in the world were born from one tiny little thought.

EXISTING AS YOU ARE

Embrace everything that you are right now and accept all the things that you are not. You are under no obligation to be anybody other than who you are. You are under no obligation to reinvent yourself for anybody. You are under no obligation to be someone else's idea of perfection.

You see, something that you should *never* forget is that the best version of you is the one that isn't trying to be something or someone else. The best version of you is the one that makes you feel whole, complete, content, *just by existing*.

The best version of you, *is you*.

PASSION

Promise yourself that you'll never stop trying when it gets hard. Promise that you won't give up on all the things you're passionate about. An abundance of greatness will present itself when your passion is embraced—and happiness will radiate from within when you're living a life that's fulfilling your soul.

HEALING

This is a reminder for anybody who is hurting right now... One day it won't hurt so much, I promise. But today it does. So cry, cry until you can't anymore, cry until you feel better. They may not be worth your tears—*but you are.* Your feelings are worth validating and your hurt is worth recognizing. Be there for yourself and let yourself feel, because letting yourself feel is *how you heal.*

MAYBE IT'S OKAY

Maybe it's okay that you haven't worked out every little detail just yet. Maybe it's okay that you're feeling a little lost lately. Maybe you don't need all the answers right now, maybe everything you need now, is right here. Maybe the only thing you're missing is trust—believing that everything will work out the way it's supposed to. Once you let go of your fears and put your trust into yourself and into the universe, that's when it all comes together. Maybe this is your sign to do it, whatever thing you're thinking of when reading this. This is your sign to trust yourself. This is your sign it's time for change.

LITTLE BY LITTLE

You'd be surprised by how many people don't have a big grand plan. So many people simply go with the flow and work everything out along the way. Don't let your lack of clear direction stop you from going anywhere, put one foot in front of the other and pave your own way. You never know what can come from taking it just one day at a time.

—*One breath, one step, one day.*

WITHIN YOU

This is your reminder that the idea of happiness that you admire in others' lives is within you too, but the thing that a lot of us don't realize is that it's not always found *in* other people. When searching for happiness you must always start from within. You must always seek out the things that make you feel like your most authentic self. You must stop comparing your life to others and create your own path that serves your highest self. You'll never convince yourself (or anyone else) that you're happy if you're not. When it's real, it's felt—not just by you but by everyone around you.

REFORMATION

It's hard to move forward before you are ready to, so be a little more patient with yourself while you are figuring out what to do next. Everything will all begin to make more sense soon. Be gentle with your healing heart and trust that sometimes things really do fall apart to make way for everything better. Do not feel like you need to rush this process and don't be let down if it's taking a little more time than you can bear with right now. Even if you are moving slowly, each day you are getting a little closer to where you need to be.

LEAP

The worst thing to regret is the thing you didn't do, when you knew all along it was what you wanted. The worst kind of regret is not trusting yourself enough to make your dreams come true.

NEXT MOVE

Keep pushing through whatever it is you're going through. Try to keep going despite what life has thrown at you—but also know that it's okay to completely break down and set your emotions free.

Even if you can't see it right now, your strength is inspiring and it will pull you through. You can't always control what life throws at you, but you can always choose your next move.

CHOOSING HAPPINESS

Happiness isn't something you simply wake up with one day. Happiness is something you have to choose—something to strive for, to work towards. You can wish for happiness, but if you rarely make choices that align with your idea of happiness, you will never truly feel it. Accept that there will be some testing moments and try a little harder to honor yourself and make decisions that better your life and your mental state. Show up for yourself first, so you can show up for others. Remember that you have to choose happiness, it doesn't always choose you. So, stay true to your idea of happiness and make a point of doing things *(no matter how small they may seem)* each day to help you achieve it.

EVOLVE

I don't know who needs to hear these words right now, but if you're not happy with something going on in your life—you're allowed to change it. You are allowed to evolve, you are allowed to move forward, you are allowed to put yourself first. Don't hold yourself back when you know that you are destined for so much more.

NEW DREAMS

It's important to trust that it's okay to leave behind an old dream to give a new dream a chance. Understand that no matter how much you try to make it work, sometimes your new dream and your old dream can't coexist for so many different reasons. It's okay to make a choice. You don't have to do everything; you don't have to please everyone. It's okay if something that previously identified you does not reflect what you want in this life anymore. People change, goals change, situations change. It's okay to be brave and leave behind what you have outgrown, it's okay to give your new dream a chance. Amazing opportunities are waiting on the other side of this decision whenever you are ready to take the leap.

WRONG TURNS

Don't strive for perfection, instead strive for gaining ex-
perience, for learning new things and stepping outside
of your comfort zone. Each wrong turn has brought you
closer to where you are now. Every mistake has given you
the knowledge you have now. Challenge yourself, give life
a go, leave this unrealistic idea of perfection behind and
accept that some chapters in your life are there to get you
to the next one. Some people in your life are there to bring
you to others. Transitioning to the next chapter is worth
making a few mistakes for. The next chapter will take you
closer to where you need to be.

SELF-SABOTAGE

If you keep telling yourself you can't do something, you are literally stopping yourself from being able to achieve it. Instead of doubting yourself, believe in yourself, back yourself, honor yourself. Stop being so influenced by your own self-doubt and fear. Go for what you want, stop sabotaging yourself and start discovering all the wonderful things you are capable of. You'll begin to see that all this time you had what it takes and more. I promise it will be worth it. I promise you'll never regret making your own dreams come true.

DREAMLAND

Everything's better when it comes from your heart, a dreamland of honesty and integrity. A place of originality and imagination, where ideas are born. Everything's better when intentions are pure and there is no fear of vulnerability. Everything's better when you let the ideas flow from within and let them inspire you instead of scare you. Let yourself dream as big as you can dream, because dreams are just the beginning. And without them, what are you living for?

NIGHT RACER

Dear Night Racer. Put your mind to rest, sweet one. I know the weight of the world feels heavy right now and even though the day has ended, you cannot seem to turn off your mind. Remember that the morning will come and so too will peace. Remember that when you wake, the worries of this moment will not feel so heavy and you'll have a chance to begin again. Give less attention to what's been and gone, and more intention for what's ahead. Slow down your mind, slow down your breaths and remember that morning will come whether you keep worrying about it or not.

LOVE NOTES TO A BROKEN HEART

Trust the process // Embrace the hurt, it is the only thing keeping you moving forward // Ground yourself, you'll be okay, it's hurting but you have the strength to fight it, you're doing great // It's going to take some time, but it's going to be okay, you are going to be okay // You may not believe it now but you're going to be so much better off from this point on // Be kind to yourself // It's okay to feel whatever you are feeling // This will pass and you will feel whole again // With time, everything will be fine // You are stronger than you realize // This is the best thing that could happen to you, you just don't know it yet // You'll love, and be loved again // You are worthy and deserving of so much more // Think about the reality of the situation rather than the fantasy // You will experience so much joy and excitement, how you feel now will pass, hang in there // You always have yourself, and you are always enough // What's meant for you won't pass you by // Process the pain, grieve, and learn the lesson // Be grateful that you were able to feel so deeply // The best is yet to come // With every heartbreak, you are one step closer to meeting the right person // Trust me, you'll be okay // Being alone is a gift that shows you how much you are worth. Embrace it // There is no timeline for healing // You are not overreacting. It's okay to feel this way. Embrace it, you'll feel a little stronger tomorrow.

OPEN HEARTED

So much beauty can come from pain
Always keep your heart open
Because what comes next is so worth it.

I'LL BE HAPPY WHEN...

You might not be exactly where you want to be, but it's so important to be grateful for what you *have at this very moment.* If you are having trouble finding gratitude for what you have right now, you may struggle to find gratitude once you achieve what you are working towards. Gratitude is essential to finding happiness and growth. Gratitude starts right here, with what you have right now.

I am grateful for _____

I am grateful for _____

I am grateful for _____

I am grateful for _____

I am grateful for _____

I am grateful for _____

I am grateful for _____

I am grateful for _____

I am grateful for _____

COMFORT

I know that it's scary taking that first leap outside of your comfort zone. The thing is though, that is exactly how you should be feeling—you are challenging yourself and that is how you grow, that is how you become the person you are meant to become. This is the beginning of a new adventure, embrace every feeling and emotion that comes with honoring yourself and your passion. You have so much opportunity ahead of this very feeling.

LOVE YOURSELF A LITTLE HARDER

If there was ever a time that you loved yourself too little, forgive yourself for accepting what you thought you deserved. Love yourself a little extra today and celebrate how far you have come, and how hard you have fought to get here. Promise yourself that you'll never forget how you deserve to be loved, treated and appreciated by others, and most importantly, by yourself.

PURPOSE

At the end of the day, I truly believe that life is all about spending your years with the people you love, doing the things you love, fulfilling your deepest passions, while falling more and more in love with yourself each and every day as you grow. When you do all things with love, you live your life with so much purpose and meaning, and that's what makes a life worth living, that's what makes it memorable, that's what makes it special.

PRESENT

I hope more than anything
that you find what you are looking for.

But please don't miss
all of the beauty along the way.

CHOOSING YOU

I hope you have the courage to choose yourself, over and over. I hope you have the courage to move forward, not backwards. To choose growth over comfort, to choose possibility over the past. I hope you know how *worthy you are* of everything you've ever wanted, even if an unkind heart has caused you to believe otherwise. Your soft heart deserves to feel *loved* and *chosen*, not just today, but *every day*. I hope you wake up each day feeling hopeful and encouraged, knowing that you're so capable of *every single thing* you want to do, big or small. I hope you remember to think beyond your comfort zone from time to time and never forget the importance of growth. I hope you remember that progression isn't always easy and sometimes the things that scare you will actually get you a lot closer to where you want to be. I hope you make the most of each day and know that *you are worthy* of the life you have been gifted, that you are worthy of success and deserve *all* the triumphs you've worked *so hard* for and all beautiful things coming your way.

MAKE IT COUNT

Making the most of each day doesn't always mean working long hours or pushing yourself too hard. Sometimes it means taking it easy if you need to rest, taking a mental health day if you are overwhelmed. Sometimes it means catching up with someone close to you if you are craving connection or taking a day trip to somewhere that makes you happy. Sometimes making the most of each day can mean just waking up, making your bed and having a shower. It doesn't mean making every minute of each day productive, it means making every minute count for something, even if it's just catching up on much needed sleep, having a nourishing meal or having a long bath. Each minute you spend taking care of yourself and doing something you love resets your soul for everything else.

OWN YOUR MIND

When you suppress the thoughts that make your mind race you only spiral yourself into all of the other thoughts you have been running from. Instead of suppressing the thoughts that make your heart beat a little faster, become more curious about them and try to understand them. Ask yourself: *Is this thought true? Why are you feeling this way? Why are you avoiding these thoughts?* I know that it's scary to confront the things you'd rather avoid, but the only way to keep these thoughts from consuming your mind is to befriend them, then you will no longer have to run in fear from your own mind.

—*I am safe to feel everything I feel.*
—*I am safe in my own mind.*

GOODNESS

There *are* people out there who would go to the end of the earth for you. There *are* people out there who would care about you so much if they were ever given a chance to get to know your kind heart. There *are* people out there who will promise you the world and actually deliver. There *are* people out there who genuinely want the absolute best for you. I know you have been hurt in the past, but please remember there *are* good souls out there who will love you with every beat of their heart. *Good people find good people,* and there is still so much good in this world to discover. I hope you have the courage to let go of your fears and stay open enough to let all the good things flow right in.

YOU ARE IN CONTROL

The thing about this way that you feel is that it's only temporary. I know that your mind is consumed right now, suffocating; it's like you can't find a way to think about anything other than the things that are causing you anxiety. These feelings don't last. It may not feel like it right now, but this feeling will fade; maybe not today, maybe not tomorrow, but you will smile again, you will feel like you again, you will feel happy and full of life again. Nothing is permanent. That's the bittersweet part about life. That's why it's so important to appreciate the truly amazing parts and people in your life while also understanding that the bad days won't last forever. Always be present, always be grateful, always know that you'll get through this obstacle and the one after that. You're so much stronger than you think you are right now. Think about it; you've gotten through every tough day in your life so far, and this is no different. Take a big breath and think of all the things you have to be grateful for and breathe out all the bad. You are in control of how you feel. You are in control of this moment.

YOU

Sometimes all you need is just one person to believe in you when nobody else does. Sometimes that's all it takes to put one foot in front of the other *even if that person is you.*

It's okay to feel
whatever you are feeling.
It's okay to not be okay.
It's okay to ask for help.
It's okay to move forward.
Your past does not define you.
Your pain does not define you.

POWERFUL LITTLE PIECES

I don't think some people realize how powerful a broken heart can be. I know that at the time it feels like your world as you know it is ending, but the journey that comes next is magical. After your heart breaks, the love for yourself that slipped away over time slowly starts to come back, because all the love you were giving to the wrong person has nowhere to go but back home to you. You slowly realize how strong you are, you learn how to make yourself happy, how to just be your own person. You laugh again, you smile again—surrounded by the people that really care about you, and you know it's genuine, you feel happy, and it's a different kind of happy to what you've felt before. You feel proud of yourself because you've pulled yourself through your lowest moment. You won't let someone take advantage of your kind heart like that again because you know better than you did before. You learn so much from your heartache, and you're never quite the same again, but in the best way possible. You can't help but feel proud of yourself because you never knew it was possible for something to get more whole when it's torn into pieces.

You'll ~~get~~ grow through
what you're going through.

MY WISH FOR YOU

There will be times that are more tough than others, times where you feel like completely giving up. Times where you worry that the life you've worked so hard for isn't the life for you after all. My only wish for you is that you don't give up no matter how tough it gets, that you believe in your purpose and what you set out to do. That you believe in your passion and know that you are worthy of the life you desire. That you believe that you are incredibly talented at what you do. My wish for you is that you never let the outside noise stray you from your true path. My dear, that is my only wish for you, no matter how tough it gets.

It's not until you stop trying to
be like everyone else that you
realize who you *truly* are.

GROWING PAINS

I know that growing can be uncomfortable but keep going. Keep growing. You are moving on from this part of your journey and into the next. Sometimes your arms can't carry everything and everyone into the next chapter. Don't shrink yourself to resist change. Spread those wings and fly to where you know you need to go to be your best self.

A MOMENT FOR FRIENDSHIP

Appreciate the ones who are there for you in the hardest moments of life, the ones who would never let you go through anything alone, the ones you can call upon and know they will be waiting with open arms to catch you before you hit the ground. *Surround* yourself with the ones who keep things lighthearted, who shine so much love on the lives of everyone around them. These friends have this endearing gift of never letting things get too serious, but somehow know exactly what you need when you need it the most. The ones who you can forget about life's worries with and enjoy each moment for exactly what it is. *Be grateful* for the ones who have moved far away, yet never for a second left your heart. The ones where each conversation begins and ends with an *I miss you* and who refuse to let the distance or time between you dwindle your connection. *Reflect upon* the friendships that you have outgrown…you know, the ones where life just got in the way, the ones that drifted away and you can't seem to remember how or why. The ones who helped you become who you are even if they aren't in your life anymore. *Treasure* the ones who are like family, the ones who are there though it all, the ones who know each and every little thing about you, the ones you trust with your whole being and love absolutely unconditionally.

MORE
SELF-LOVE

LESS
SELF-DOUBT

DISCONNECTED MOMENTS

It's normal to have moments where all you want to do is disconnect from the world. You don't have to feel 'on' all of the time. You're allowed to have a break to recharge. You're allowed to look after yourself.

—*Give yourself permission to rest*

I'M PROUD OF YOU

Just in case no one has told you this today, I'm so proud of you and everything you have endured and achieved. I hope you know how worthy you are and how much you bring to the world.

I'm proud of you for not giving up, no matter how many times you've wanted to. I'm proud of you for choosing to keep going. I'm proud of you for continuing to show up each day despite what you have been through.

I'm proud of you for taking steps to better yourself and your life lately and for finally showing yourself just how much you are capable of.

Your strength and courage is inspiring, and you should be so proud of yourself, too.

THE FUNNY THING ABOUT CLOSURE

The funny thing about closure is that you're never really sure exactly when it will come. It's one of those things you intentionally search for, yet it usually comes when you least expect it. It may feel like closure is impossible to find one day, then there it is, the very next day, appearing out of nowhere. All of a sudden, a wave of comfort flows through your body and everything makes sense. That's why you need to remember that it's possible and it's coming for you, just be patient and trust that everything is as it should be, even if it doesn't make perfect sense right now, or at all. Also remember that sometimes closure finds you simply in the way of moving forward, without explanations, without all the answers, and it's still just as beautiful.

At some point in your life
you may need to let go of
someone you love in
order to love yourself
the way you deserve to be loved.

THE JOURNEY TO SELF-WORTH

You should never let how people feel about you dictate the way that you feel about yourself. It's so common to measure your self-worth by external factors and it's not until you truly value yourself that you learn how heart-breaking that is. Why is it that some people can so easily make you feel like you're not good enough, or that you're not worthy of what they have to offer? How can the way someone feels about you make you doubt yourself and destroy your confidence? Stop letting shitty people dictate how you feel about yourself. Stop letting people who have a long way to go with their personal development hinder your progression. When will you realize just how much you deserve? When will you see that you are so worthy of what you desire? When will you stop looking for validation in the wrong places? When will you realize that it's all in you. It always has been and it always will be.

INTUITION

If you're feeling unsure about whether or not you can trust someone, the best person to trust is yourself.

SUN RAYS

I just want to take a moment to tell whoever is reading this right now that even on your hardest days, you are so much stronger than what you give yourself credit for, you are so much more incredible than you realize, you are pure sunshine and you make the lives of all the people around you better, *just by being you.*

A step by step guide
on how to be the
best version of yourself.

STEP 1: Decide that you are
enough just as you are.

CERTAINTY

Please don't be so afraid of not getting things right the first time or of making the wrong decision. Sometimes you need to make the wrong decision only to realize that it's not what you want. Some hearts need certainty before they move on from someone or something, and sometimes it's hard to move forward with unanswered questions. It's okay to learn by messing up, it's okay to take things one step at a time and move forward with caution. Pay attention to the revelations that follow on from the decisions that don't feel right as there is always so much growth on the other side of them.

GENEROUS HEART

The way you love even after you've been broken is one of the most endearing things about you. The way that you give out pieces of your heart even after it's been stolen before is what makes you so special.

FEEL IT ONCE MORE

I hope you discover something you love so much that you throw yourself so deeply into it without a second thought. I hope you get to experience that no-hesitation, have-to-have-it, all-or-nothing, unconditional kind of love. The kind of passion that makes the blood flowing through your body feel electric. I hope you get to experience the kind of passion that makes you so excited you struggle to find your words when you talk about it, because words don't even come close to explaining the way it feels. I hope that no matter what you have been through, no matter who has hurt you or how many times you have failed, you remember this feeling, and fight to feel it once more. Because life is meant to be lived, life is meant to be felt, the pleasure, the pain and *everything in-between.*

THE ONE

Isn't it fascinating that the way we view love can change because of the actions of just *one* person, for better or for worse. *One* person can hurt you so much that you never want to love again, *one* person can treat your heart so poorly that you decide it's easier to not feel love at all. *One* person can destroy too much. The thing is, *one* person does not define your worth, *one* person does not define how you deserve to be treated or loved, *one* person does not define how you love others. *One* person does not get to hold this much power over your heart, *one* person does not get to hold this much power over your future. Please keep your heart open for the *one* person that's going to love you softly, deeply, passionately, patiently, kindly. Please keep your heart open for the *one* person who has the potential to *change it all.*

MEND

Thank you for teaching me that I was wasting my time on an *"I can't do this anymore"* kind of love, when all I ever wanted was a *"we've got this, let's fix this"* kind of love.

Never apologize
for how much you feel,
for how much you hurt,
for how much you love.

FLUTTER

This is for anybody
with a healing heart
one day you will find
exactly what you deserve
so don't change
the rhythm of your heart
for anyone.

INWARD

One of the most heartbreaking ways to damage your confidence and destroy your gratitude is to live each day comparing your life with everyone else's. If you are looking for the answers in anyone other other than yourself, then you are looking in the wrong place. What you do is enough, what you have is enough, who you are is enough. Look inward, focus on yourself and your achievements, worry less about the outside noise. Dream big, but don't let your thoughts wander so far away from you that you get stuck and place unrealistic expectations upon yourself.

CORNERS

The road to *'success'* isn't always uphill. There are ups, there are downs, corners you don't see coming and speed bumps that come out of nowhere. Sometimes you can even go around in circles. But you keep going. You don't give up. And that's what separates you from failure, because you know it isn't an option.

Take some time today to
recognize where you are right now
and how hard you've worked to
get there, even if you're not exactly
where you dream to be just yet.

When you search for happiness
exclusively in another soul,
it will never truly be yours to hold.

The only happiness
you can be sure belongs to you
Is the one you find within yourself.

A BEAUTIFUL MESS

It's a mess but it's a beautiful one. That's the thing about healing. The end result is beautiful but the process is anything but. Healing is messy. It is confronting, confusing, conflicting, yet completely transformative. There is no timeline, you will heal precisely when you are ready to. Don't give up just as it gets messy, because that is when the real work is done. Be patient and gentle with yourself in the process. Tell yourself that it *does* get better, day by day, even if you can't see it or feel it right now. Sometimes you need to reopen an old wound to make peace with it, to accept that it is part of who you are, and to trust that it does not define where you are heading.

'FOREVER'

Accepting that it's time to move on from what you thought was your forever is one of the hardest things to do. Nothing in life is promised and sometimes even the things that you were *so* sure you were destined for can fall apart in your hands. Maybe you saw it coming and you were trying with all your strength to hold on even though you knew you should just let go, or maybe you didn't see it coming *at all*. One thing you must know is that no matter how it happened, no matter how much you are hurting, there is *always* light after the dark.

I know it's hard to heal from something you wanted so deeply, it's hard to move on from a situation you so desperately wanted to be your forever.

But maybe your 'forever' was never meant to be your 'forever' after all. Maybe your 'forever' was only meant to be temporary. Maybe your 'forever' was always supposed to be your biggest lesson. Maybe losing your 'forever' could be the best thing that ever happens to you.

What if you heal from this messiness and find everything you were looking for? What if everything is working out the way it was always supposed to and you'll look back on this pain and pinpoint the exact moment that everything began to fall into place?

PATIENCE

Find curiosity in the waiting.
Find curiosity in not knowing.
Find curiosity in wondering what comes next.
Find curiosity in the process.
Be curious in all parts of your journey.

If someone is *hurting* you
more than they are *healing* you,
maybe it's time to *let them go*.

NEW FUTURES

Sometimes you *need* to
let go of the people you
love because they do *not*
want the same things as *you*.

As hard as it can be, sometimes you need to decide it's time
to let go of one version of your future, to give *yourself* the
future you have always imagined and deserved. The people
you choose throughout this life are not always meant for
you. Not because you don't adore them, but because your
paths don't align. As hard as it is, please don't give up *all*
of who you are or what you have *always* wanted, purely
to make a life work for someone else. Compromise where
you can but never give up your dreams or your identity to
make yourself fit into someone else's idea of a perfect life.
Don't betray yourself like that, because darling, you deserve
so much more.

DO IT FOR YOU

Make sure you are doing it for *you*.
Whatever it is that you are doing,
Whatever it is you wish to do,
Always make sure that you are doing it for *you*.

MEANINGFUL

What can you do *right now*
to make this day count?

What small steps can you take to make this day mean
something more than the last? What can you do to use
this day to get you closer to where you want your life to end
up? The days can pass so quickly without creating anything
meaningful, and too many meaningless days will eventually
contribute to a meaningless life.

You know deep down in your passionate heart that you
were put on this earth for so much more than a mediocre
life. So ask yourself what small thing you can do today to
get yourself more prepared for tomorrow, more prepared for
your future. The time for making excuses ends now.

Do something right now even if it's small. Show yourself that you care about your future, show yourself what you are capable of.

Read that book you've been wanting to read, have that conversation you have been avoiding, write that list you've been meaning to write, apply for that job you know you're qualified for, start that passion project, put the wheels in motion even if they are moving slowly.

Take one bold step forward with all the passion in your body and throw away the self-doubt that has held you back for far too long. You can do this, you are capable. Whatever it is that you are thinking of when reading this, go and do it.

ALIGNMENT

When your head and your heart align, that is when the magic happens. When you find that sweet spot where everything makes sense and inspires you at the same time, that is when you know it's going in the right direction, and more importantly, *coming from the right place.* When this happens, please just go for it and do not hold back. Once you find this alignment, no idea is too far fetched, the 'what if' turns into 'why not', and it's because you have full trust in your head, full trust in your heart, and full trust in the universe. The late nights don't feel so late because you're proud of what you are creating, the hours fly by because you are so immersed in your passion. You're happy. You're content. Because finally it all makes sense and you're ready to take that next step without the self-doubt tempting you to retreat back into your comfort zone like it so often does. When your passion takes over there is nothing that can stop it, so just go with it, let it take you where you need to go, it's now or never…

WORTHY

When the love is right and the person is right, it will work out. Trust that. Believe that. Stop doubting yourself and questioning your self-worth. If someone is making you feel that you are less than worthy then that is not the right person for you. You deserve to feel loved and adored, just the way you are.

DECEPTION

Be kind to your mind. You were not born with the darkest and most difficult thoughts that you have about yourself. These thoughts often arise by the actions of those who do not deserve your love. If we try to navigate the world with these unhelpful thoughts at the forefront of our minds, eventually, we begin to believe them and allow them to consume us which redirects us from our true potential.

Stop deceiving your own mind.
Stop hurting your own heart.

BEYOND BELIEF

Why is it that you believe in the ones you love
so effortlessly and *unconditionally* yet struggle to
give *yourself* that same hope and optimism?

Think about it, no matter what they do, you genuinely be-
lieve in their ability and capability and know that whatever
they choose to do with their life will be an absolute success.
Now imagine how differently you would feel if you treated
yourself in that same way. Imagine if you instinctively, un-
conditionally, wholeheartedly believed in our own ability
and capability and didn't let self-doubt or low confidence get
in the way of your dreams. Just imagine what you would do,
how you would feel, where you could go and what you would
be able to achieve if you just trusted yourself like you trust
others. Because I'm telling you right now, everyone around
you believes you have what it takes; everyone but you.

I just wish more
than anything
that you could see yourself
the same way the
world sees you.

AS YOU GROW

As you grow, you will begin to feel content with some of the things you can't possibly imagine right now. You will learn to enjoy your own company as much as you enjoy the company of others, you will wake up on a Sunday morning, make a coffee for yourself, and be proud of where you are and how much you've accomplished. As you grow, you will become more comfortable with looking inwards and focusing on yourself more than others, because you have finally realized that no one can get you to where you want to be but you. As you grow, you will start to see that it was never selfish putting yourself first and that everything you've ever needed, you've had all along—you just needed to love yourself a little harder to give yourself the chance to find it. As you grow, you realize that there truly is no competition as we are all so wonderfully unique, and that the best person you can be in any situation is yourself. The most valuable lesson of all is that we each have to walk our own paths at our own pace. I know it's hard to picture it because I struggled to see it too. Please trust that this calmness will find you. I just want you to know it's out there waiting for you because I wish someone had told me this. It's funny the way life works. We always want the answers so desperately that we forget it's all a journey. So learn as much as you can from this moment because I promise that you will look back on these days in years to come and realize that those moments were teaching you so much more than what you realized at the time, and those moments were always meant to be part of your journey to get you right where you always needed to be.

THE COMFORT-FREE ZONE

The thing is, sometimes you must do the things you think you can't. I know it's hard, believe me I do, but that's how you continue to move forward and get ahead. The things you think you can't do are the very things holding you back. The truth is, you need to overcome these challenges to continue to grow. You must escape your place of comfort for anything to change. Sometimes you need to get uncomfortable to achieve the things you think you can't.

Remember to acknowledge all achievements
big or small, whenever you can.

PUSH

Sometimes things happen
before you are ready
for them to happen.

It doesn't mean the timing is wrong, sometimes it means
the timing is just right and the universe knows you are ready
and that maybe you just needed that extra push in the right
direction to get you on your way. Embrace this new journey
with everything you are. Everything is unfolding exactly
how it's supposed to, even if you can't see it like that just yet.

HERE

You exist.
You are here.
No matter what you are feeling right now
You exist, and you are here.

—*Things to be grateful for.*

POTENTIAL

Have you ever experienced the pain of falling in love with someone—not because of who they are but because of who they could be, because of who they would be if they lived up to their promises, if they lived up to their words, if they had a heart like yours. It hurts to see so much potential in someone who has no desire to be the person you know they are worthy of becoming. If you have experienced this before, I want you to know that you deserve someone who is everything you need, someone who keeps their promises, someone who has more than just potential. You deserve someone who follows through, you deserve to have every little bit of energy you put in, given back. You deserve it all.

LIMITS

You can get through the most challenging of seasons and you can get through the things you think you can't. You have been tested to the absolute limit before and found a way to get through it. You are so much stronger than you think you are, and you have pulled yourself through it all. *You are resilient.*

HEALING HEARTS

I hope that every heart
finds an *authentic* love.

The kind of love that doesn't hurt, the kind of love that
doesn't make you feel inadequate, the kind of love that feels
like forever. I hope that every healing heart knows that they
are worthy of this love, and they always have been, it's just
the wrong kind of people who have made you feel like your
love is not enough.

UNAPOLOGETIC HEARTS

Never apologize for how much love you have in your heart. Never apologize for letting someone take advantage of that. Never apologize for hurting when it hurts. Never apologize for somebody else's inability to love you the way you deserve to be loved.

You don't have to feel productive
one hundred percent of the time.
It's okay to take a break.

FLOW

Pay attention to the things that make you feel whole, feel happy, feel alive…and then do more of those things. Connect with nature, practice gratitude, journal morning or night, get more sunlight, go for more walks, learn something new. Don't force productivity or creativity, let everything flow naturally from your heart. Forgive yourself if things don't go as you hoped or planned and remind yourself that *you are human*. Don't dwell on what could have been, always let that energy go and keep moving forward. Be realistic with the expectations you put on yourself and remember that some things *can* actually wait. Never forget that you are a priority and so worthy of your time.

WHEN THE HEAD MEETS THE HEART

Isn't it interesting how you can miss someone with every single beat of your heart yet still know in the depths of your soul that you are better off without them? I'm not sure if you can force yourself to get past that feeling, that feeling of missing someone you know you *can't*, or *shouldn't* have. What I do know is that the miscommunication between the head and the heart can leave you feeling torn, lost, confused, trying to move forward without knowing if it's even the right thing to do. In my experience, the heart can take a little longer to catch up with your head, especially when it comes to getting familiar with the new, and moving on from someone you once loved, *or maybe still do*. Why does the heart have this natural desire to hold onto anyone who has taken residency there? Be gentle with yourself, this is all new and you are doing the best you can to navigate it all. Maybe your heart is holding on a little longer because it knows that you're not ready to forget just yet, maybe you haven't learned what you were supposed to learn from this just yet. I believe that there is a lesson in each soul you love, love is never wasted, and neither is this pain.

LIGHT

Focus on the light, not the dark.

You can't let the one negative in a
sea of positives hold power over you.

CHOSEN

*What does it mean
to choose yourself?*

It means finally putting *your* needs before the needs of *other* people who don't value you. It means putting boundaries in place that protect you and your mental health. It means making decisions that actually benefit you instead of making decisions in another attempt to people-please. It means believing in yourself, loving yourself and trusting yourself. It means standing up for yourself and what you believe in. It means focusing on the positives and possibilities instead of the negatives and hesitations. It means letting go of people who are not holding you as tight as you need them to. It means taking a break when you feel yourself burning out. It means truly accepting yourself for everything that you are, and believing that you deserve only the best.

EVOLUTION

Have you ever felt like everything around you is changing before you are ready for it to change? It's hard to explain, it's almost like you are happy with your life the way it is but everyone around you is changing at a different pace and you're not quite ready to keep up with it yet. You feel the rug ripped right from underneath you and feel like you are losing control. The important thing to remember is that you can't control something that was *never yours* to control. This is when you begin to learn that it is time to focus on yourself. This phase of your life is all about you, this journey you are about to begin is when you'll learn about all the things that hold purpose for you, and what you want your life to look like. This is when you'll learn that it was never about other people and their life plans, it's all about you. You'll learn to accept that life moves at a different pace for every individual on this planet *and that's okay.* Do not let this feeling make you grow cynical or believe that you are not worthy of everything you so undeniably want in life. Just because someone has reached that point in their journey before you, it doesn't mean it's not there waiting *for you too.* Do not force things to happen purely because you feel like you need to keep up, *that's doing things for the wrong reason.* Always lead with love and integrity and trust that you will reach your milestones in perfect time—and it won't be any less meaningful *even if it takes you a little longer.*

HUMAN

Even the people you look up to feel a little lost sometimes. Even the people you look up to doubt themselves. Even the people you look up to have days where they feel like they failed. Even the people you look up to have moments where they don't trust themselves. Even the people you look up to need to be reminded of their beauty and their gift. Even the people you look up to need positive affirmations and words of encouragement. Even the people you look up to are human. *Allow yourself to be human too.*

MESSY MOMENTS

When life gets uncomfortable and the messiness begins to show, all you can do is be the best version of yourself you can be. I hope you have the strength to open yourself up to the discomfort and the courage to handle yourself in the unfamiliar moments. Remember that you can't control the situation and you can't control the outcome. What you can control is how you choose to show up through the messy moments in life.

EVERYTHING, *ALL AT ONCE*

You might not be exactly where you want to be, but look at how far you have come. Don't let the pressure you put on yourself to be everything *all at once* steal your brain space. You don't have to be anything more than who you are right now, because who you are is *enough*. Free your mind of anything ahead of you that is not relevant to this moment. Take a deep breath and try to put everything into perspective.

You do not have to be everything all at once.

FORGIVING

Sometimes you can go through the same situations over and over again until you *finally* decide you want to do things differently. Please don't punish yourself for taking your time to figure it all out, and be sure to forgive yourself for the mistakes you made while you were growing.

SOMEONE LIKE YOU

I hope you find the person
Who makes you feel like yourself,
Who makes you genuinely happy.
I hope you find the person
Who is looking for someone
Just like you.

SUNSHINE AND RAIN

Let one bad day be one bad day. Life isn't sunshine all of the time, *that's just the way it is.* You can't let one bad day or one bad moment hold so much power over you. We tend to shift our focus when bad things happen which is so heartbreaking because when we do that we forget about all the beauty we have to be thankful for. Next time you have a bad day, pause and remember all of the good things you have in this moment with you, remember all the people you have there to support you and all the hope you have ahead. Let all of the goodness in your life carry you through the times that are a little darker than others. Life isn't sunshine all the time but remember that you have so much light within you and around you, and it's there for you whenever you need it.

ONE FOOT IN FRONT OF THE OTHER

One of the hardest things to do is to move forward without all of the answers. Sometimes you need to move on not exactly knowing why—and be okay with that. Maybe closure is *actually* really all about *you*. You are the one who chooses to put one foot in front of the other each day, no one else can do that for you. So maybe it *is* possible to move forward—even when the reasons *why* are a mystery. Closure is not something we are all fortunate enough to get, so trust that you have the strength to get yourself through this season, with or without the answers. Maybe the answers will come one day in the future, *once you are ready to see them.*

UNCONDITIONAL

When the love is unconditional there really isn't anything that can come between it. It's a beautiful thing, unconditional love. That's what it means to be loved fully for everything you are, to be accepted, forgiven, embraced, and celebrated in every way. When you are loved and show love in this way, you are free. Free to be yourself, to make mistakes, to learn and to grow as a human being and be accepted through all parts of your journey. Love shouldn't restrict you, it should set you free. I hope you find a love that lets you grow and be vulnerable without fear of judgment or abandonment.

ACCEPTANCE

Sometimes you need to let go and accept things the way they are, and not the way you wished they could be. Some parts of your journey are only supposed to be temporary. Maybe this is part of your journey to teach you a lesson, to teach you that you deserve more, to encourage you to grow.

AMBIGUITY

Have you ever experienced that feeling in your heart when you know that something in your life is not quite right? Maybe you're not completely happy with how things are right now or you're constantly holding onto this hope that things won't always be this way because you know you're destined for so much more. It's easy to ignore that feeling and continue existing in your life as it is, but I don't think it ever really goes away unless you do something about it, unless you make a change. Let this be your sign. That feeling is telling you something that you already know, follow that feeling to where it's meant to take you.

HANDLE WITH CARE

In moments of darkness, please don't forget your worth. Whatever you're going through, or have been through, does not change the way the world sees and loves you, and nor should it change the way you see and love yourself. Don't forget to be compassionate with yourself and handle yourself with care when your world around you feels heavy. Be patient with yourself, there is no need to rush when you are healing.

—Please come home to yourself when you are ready.

BELONGING

I hope you find people in this life who make you feel like you are meant to be here, who make you feel like you belong exactly *as you are*. I hope you find the kind of people who calm your soul when you see their face or hear their voice. I hope you surround yourself with the kind of people who make you feel like there is nowhere else you'd rather be in this world *than right here with them*.

I also hope you find this in yourself too. I hope you know that you belong here, exactly as you are.

Always hold onto hope.
Hope gives us so much to live for,
to hold out for, to hold onto.

GRAVITATION

Whatever you do, please don't shrink yourself to resist the change you are longing for. Please don't let the weight of other people hold you down to the point where you're unable to move forward at all. Listen to your heart, open up your mind and gravitate to where you know in your heart you need to be. Move away from anyone or anything in your life that is making you feel like you need to be someone *you're not*. Move closer to the people and the things that make your heart dance with happiness. Life is too short to live a life that doesn't feel like *yours*.

The moment you ask yourself
if you deserve better
is the very moment
you realize you do.

And all this time
you thought
you were falling apart,

you didn't realize
you were actually
putting yourself
back together.

—healing

THE BEST KIND OF PEOPLE

The best kind of people are the ones who love you unconditionally, are soft and gentle with your heart and soul, make you smile with just their presence, know when something is not right without you having to say anything at all, take responsibility for their actions, respect other humans, let you be yourself, accept you as you are, forgive others instead of seeking revenge, are patient with your struggles, are there no matter the situation, make you feel safe, loved, and understood, help you without expecting something in return, listen attentively, ask you to message them when you get home safe, are there for you during the lows just as much as the highs, check up on you when you are quieter, are honest and believe in lifting other people up, focus on self-care, see the best in you even when you can't, teach you new things, find happiness in your happiness, show you that you are loved and reassure you when you need it, don't try to make you feel guilty for being upset, are always kind, hold space for you to feel your feelings without judgment, are present with you, bring sunshine to your day.

BALANCE

When you feel yourself losing control,
put more focus on the things you can control
rather than the things you cannot.

You cannot control the way people feel about you,
but you can control the way you feel about yourself.

You cannot control the way someone loves you,
but you can control the way you love yourself.

You cannot control the way others value you,
But you can control the way you value yourself.

You cannot control the outcome of a situation,
but you can control how you react.

I am in awe of you
and the way you keep going
regardless of how many times
you have asked yourself if you should.

I am proud of you
for putting it all on the line
for believing in yourself enough
to find what your heart is looking for.

—Vulnerability

NEW BEGINNINGS

I know that moving forward isn't easy, but I also know that it's possible. I know your heart might not be ready to let go just yet, but I also know that it's necessary. I know that you're wondering if you will find happiness again, but I also know that you can. I know that it's hard to see past this moment, but this moment is not forever. If people can be temporary in our lives, *then so too can feelings*. Feel everything you need to feel at this moment, as this feeling is necessary for your healing. Hold onto the hope that you can carry yourself through this pain and uncertainty, until the days feel a little brighter and your soul feels a little lighter.

Spend more time with the people
who remind you who you are.

Don't run from your potential

just because you are scared

in the space between

where you are now

and where

you want to be.

The day you realize
that comparing yourself
to those around you
gets you absolutely nowhere
is the day you set yourself free.

Consume less.

Create more.

Overthink less.

Dream more.

Worry less.

Pause more.

Criticize less.

Appreciate more.

Doubt less.

Go for more.

Force less.

Flow more.

Control less.

Accept more.

Carry less.

Release more.

Suppress less.

Feel more.

Hate less.

Love more.

Scroll less.

Live more.

RESISTANCE

One of the hardest truths to swallow is the realization that sometimes there isn't an opponent, sometimes the only person working against you right now is you. Stop running in the opposite direction of opportunity whenever you are scared. Stop turning backwards because it's the easiest thing to do. Stop finding comfort in the past, in what's familiar. Open up your heart and trust that the real magic begins to happen when you finally realize that you are the only person standing between yourself and your potential, between where you are now and where you need to be.

—*The opposite of pursuing your dreams is avoiding them.*

ANGELS

Remember that the ones we love
Can live within our hearts
As long as we need them to
Even if they are no longer here.

22 REASONS TO LOVE YOURSELF

Your willingness to help people. The way you continue to fight when you want to give up. Your kindness and empathy. Your open mind and ability to understand others. Your persistence and forgiving heart. Your resilience and compassion. The way you manage to make everyone feel comfortable. Your ability to love fully even if your heart is on the line. The way you find a way to see the good in others. Your optimism and positivity, even in the toughest of situations. The way your authenticity shines through everything you do. Your passion and determination. The way you continue to care about others even if they have let you down. Your loyalty and strength. Your ability to grow from every challenge you have faced. Your selflessness and your gentleness. Your ability to always see from another's' perspective. Your ability to be the friend that everyone needs. The way you make time to listen to others when they need it. The way you show up for yourself when you find something you are passionate about. Your honesty and ability to do all things with love. The way you try to be the best version of yourself each day.

Just a reminder
that there is no rush
it doesn't matter
how long it takes
what matters is that
you get there
in one piece.

ONE PERSON

Sometimes all you really need is just one person. One person who understands you entirely, one person who you can share your thoughts with safely, with trust and without judgment. One person who won't give up on you, nor you on them—no matter how tough things get. Sometimes all you really need is someone to just be there, not necessarily doing anything or saying anything, but to just be there when you need them. Sometimes the words "I've got you" are all you need to hear to keep going. As you grow you really do realize that quality is far greater than quantity, and these friendships must be treasured. So hold onto them with everything you've got and make sure they always know that *you've got them too.*

JUST FOR NOW

I know this may seem like the hardest thing to believe right now, but your heart won't feel this heavy forever and someday soon this pain won't feel so overbearing. But just for now, take a deep breath and feel everything you are feeling. Open your arms and carry yourself with care.

—*You are healing and that is beautiful.*

SUNSHINE SOULS

This is a little reminder that the light you bring to the world is needed so much more in times of darkness. Please keep sharing your generous heart without fear. There are so many people out there who rely on the magic you create and the kindness you spread. You could be the reason someone smiles today, the reason someone pauses and takes a deep breath. You never know who needs to be touched by a heart like yours, so please keep spreading your light.

Invest in yourself,
your future self is worth it.

ADJUSTMENT

I think it's important to remember that when you make life-altering decisions it's normal to feel sad and confused afterwards. Feeling this way does not mean you made the wrong decision, it just means that you need some time to re-adjust. Trust yourself and trust your decision.

BEING YOU

Be the person who cares, even if it's too much. Be the person who loves, be the person who sees the good in each soul you cross paths with. Be the person who spreads kindness. Be the person who checks in on the people who haven't been themselves lately. Be the person who sends a text to someone close to you to let them know you're thinking of them. Be the person who makes your loved ones feel important and appreciated each day. Be the person who listens, someone who understands, someone who is genuinely happy for the people around them, be someone who doesn't hold others back, but encourages them to grow and be everything they dream to be. Be the person who helps the people you care about without hesitation, and who doesn't expect anything in return. Be the person you know you are even though you have been hurt before by being exactly as you are, by being too loving, too caring, too available, too much. Be the person you were born to be and do not let the actions of others take away at the most beautiful qualities you could ever find in a person. Be the person who believes that the only way to attract all the people who are meant for you is to be exactly who you are.

LOVE LANGUAGE

If you have found yourself needing to spell out all the ways you deserve to be loved, you might be giving your heart away to the wrong person. You deserve to be loved by someone who speaks the language of your heart and can read your soul without you needing to spell it out word for word.

—You were never asking for too much for wanting to be loved in the same way you love, you were simply asking for your love to be returned in the way you deserve.

PLEASER

You call yourself a people pleaser yet you don't recall the last time you pleased yourself. *I hope you're not forgetting that you're a person worth pleasing too.*

A MOMENT TO BREATHE

This is your reminder that your comfort zone serves a purpose but it's not your *permanent* home. Your comfort zone is a place for you to recoup and take a moment to breathe, but it can get stagnant there. When you get too comfortable there it's easy to lose the motivation needed for new ideas and new opportunities to come to life. The truth is, we all need to do things that we're not comfortable with, things we don't want to do, because we know it's imperative to grow, to heal, to progress and to do all the things that make life *mean something*. While it's tempting to live in a constant state of comfort, it's important to remember that it's easy to get too cozy and get stuck there. Remember that you don't need to leave your comfort zone in one great big, giant leap of faith, you can take small but mighty steps, little by little, until you're ready to walk right into your next chapter. Be assured that your comfort zone will always be there for you to come back to and you can re-enter anytime you need to, just make a conscious effort to step out every now and then or you'll never get the chance to experience all the beautiful moments that are meant for you.

Don't allow your self-doubt
to make your choices for you.
You can't let your fears
dictate your future.

And then
all of a sudden
without even realizing
every single sacrifice
you have ever made
and every single set back
along the way
began to make sense.

—perseverance

5 REASONS TO PRIORITIZE YOURSELF

You Are Your Biggest Commitment. You're with yourself for life. To be able to give yourself that life you really deserve, you need to learn that you are your biggest commitment, and you deserve to put the same effort into yourself as you put into others. It might feel selfish at first but it's not, I promise.

When you prioritize yourself, your personal boundaries are protected. What we sometimes don't realize is that we teach others how to treat us based on how we treat ourselves. When you become more comfortable with putting yourself first, you respect your personal boundaries so much more, which means they are respected by others. When we don't value ourselves or our boundaries, it can seem like no one else does either which can leave you feeling frustrated, undervalued, and unheard. The truth is, protecting your boundaries is entirely up to you. Setting healthy boundaries for yourself is important and implementing them is even more important. Don't feel guilty about doing this. The people who respect you, will respect your boundaries.

You Are Worthy. Read it again. *You are worthy.*

You are worthy of your love, your efforts, your hopes, your dreams, healthy relationships, you are worthy of it all. Self-worth is important. If you truly believe that you are not worthy, then that is exactly what you will attract and manifest. You should never let your negative self-talk take over and make you feel like you are not worthy of each and every single thing that you desire.

The longer you neglect yourself, the harder it becomes to prioritize yourself. Don't condition yourself and others to believe that you don't deserve to be a priority in your own life. There are a lot of people who will try and take what they can get from a person or a situation, and the longer you allow this to continue, the more likely it is to happen. It is up to you to protect yourself from this, it is up to you to change your narrative.

When you're at your best, you can give your best—to yourself and to others. If you keep giving more than what you have, you are teaching yourself that your needs don't matter, you are depleting yourself of everything you are and everything you have, and this is how you lose yourself.

THANK YOU FOR *NOT* BEING EVERYTHING I WANTED YOU TO BE

Thank you for not being everything I wanted you to be. Thank you for showing me how to love fiercely and unconditionally. Thank you for letting me experience that euphoric feeling of falling, foolishly hoping once more that this could be it. Thank you for showing me the hardships of relationships and teaching me compromise and sacrifice, and that it's not always as "easy" as it seems. Thank you for teaching me what I really wanted in a relationship and life partner. Thank you for what you taught me about myself, for all the things I never knew or never realized. Thank you for showing me that even though I wasn't perfect I was still deserving of love and happiness. Thank you for teaching me how to pull myself back up, how to be okay when I don't feel okay. Thank you for showing me that it's okay if things don't go to plan, if things turn out differently, if your future suddenly becomes your past. Thank you for showing me that it's possible to love again, and harder than before, and that maybe there is more than just the one person out there for me. Thank you for breaking my heart, thank you for not being everything I wanted you to be, so I could find someone that is.

—*To anyone who has hurt my heart.*

Always prioritize
the person you are
over the person
who makes you
question who you are.

THINGS YOU PROBABLY WON'T REGRET

Studying more. Reading more books. Drinking more water. Making new friends. Being more honest. Following your passion. Going to bed early. Meditating more. Quitting a job you absolutely hate. Being kind to a stranger. Taking a break when you need one. Listening to your heart. Looking after your body. Crying when you need to. Putting yourself first. Leaving your comfort zone when you need to. Hugging someone you love. Going on more adventures. Accepting your imperfections. Telling your loved ones how much you care about them. Understanding your emotions. Going to therapy. Taking care of your mental health. Trusting your intuition. Letting go of toxic people. Finding your purpose. Loving yourself more.

HEALING WITH WORDS

If writing is what brings you peace, then write until your pen runs out, write until there are no pages left and let each sentence soothe your soul. Stop judging yourself and what you write, not everything has to be a poetic masterpiece, sometimes just getting your thoughts on paper can validate your emotions and make more sense of them so you are able to clear your mind, *even if just for a moment*. Sometimes laying your life out on a piece of paper is the most cathartic experience you can have.

Be gentle with yourself
on the days you are
feeling everything.
Be gentle with yourself
on the days you are
feeling nothing.
Be gentle with yourself
through whatever you are
feeling right now.

PURE INTENTIONS

This is a reminder for anyone who is doubting themselves right now; do what you do best and do it with pride, do it without worrying about what anyone else thinks, do it without holding back, do it with *all of your heart.* The second you start to ruminate on the opinions of those around you is the second you start to overthink and question your work, your worth, and your purpose.

LET GO

If there is anyone or anything in your life that is making you feel like you need to be someone you're not, maybe they are not meant to be in your life.

—*Life is too short to play pretend.*

SELF-BELIEF

Think about the people you look up to. Then think about what they have that you don't. You'd be surprised at how capable you are of doing everything you think you can't. Have a little faith in yourself and shoot for the stars.

HOME

Sometimes *'home'* is simply a feeling; a feeling of belonging *right where you are*, even if where you are is the furthest from home you have ever been.

PERSEVERANCE

I am sorry if your heart is hurting more than you are able to cope with right now. I am sorry if someone has disregarded your feelings and left you feeling this way. Life can be unfair, trust that this pain doesn't last forever. You will never be dealt a hand you can't play.

CLOSURE

I think you realize
that you're letting go
when all the words
that were meant for them
fill the pages
of your notebook instead.

DESERVING

No matter what you are healing from right now, I hope you always know that you deserve to find happiness, feel love, and be appreciated by the ones you choose to surround yourself with.

Please don't live your life
believing that
you are unlovable
just because somebody has
fallen out of love with you
in the past.

Please don't live your life
believing that
your worth is defined
by the one person
who did not hold your heart
the way it deserved to be held.

STAR-GAZER

Ask yourself what you want your life to look like. Close your eyes and try to picture yourself living your happiest life, to the highest potential. Notice what surrounds you, who surrounds you. Notice what you have and what you bravely left behind to get to this place of peace. Now think about the present moment and ask yourself if the life you are living now will eventually lead you to the life you were just imagining for yourself. And if the answer is no, ask yourself what you could do differently.

GO

All it takes is the courage to just say yes.
Everything else can fall into place later.
For now all you need to do is *begin*.

REDIRECT

The path you have traveled all this time does not need to define where you are going. I know that it is daunting to change your path, but as humans we change our minds all the time and that is okay. One of the bravest things you can do is decide you want better for yourself and actually act on it. Be bold, be brave.

—You've got this.

BABY STEPS

I know that you know your heart deserves better, I know that you want to move forward. I know it's hard to pretend all your feelings aren't there and simply do what your head is telling you to do but I also know how hard that is. I want you to know that it's okay to move at a pace that makes you feel comfortable. You don't need all the answers right now. Right now, all you need to know is that it will be okay, *you will be okay.*

You deserve better than the one
who isn't taking notice of you.

WHOLE AGAIN

When your heart has been broken it is hard to imagine yourself feeling whole again, and then all of a sudden you're laughing until your rib cage hurts with friends you never would have made if it didn't all end up the way that it did. Life is good, and even though it isn't perfect it sure is beginning to make a lot more sense.

—*Perspective*

SOULMATES

Some souls *instantly* click. Whether you're lovers, best friends, soulmates, or something so special that words *can't quite explain it*. You accept this person for *everything* they are, and they would never let you be anything other than your beautiful, *imperfect self*. These are the souls that you encounter and just know in the very first moment that you were *supposed* to cross paths. Their presence makes you feel safe and calm, like you are home whenever you're with *them*. They are *without a doubt* the most special person you've had the privilege to love—no distance, time, or person could come between the bond you share. Their kindness, softness, sincerity, and unconditional love makes you feel like a better person, because life is simply better *with them in it*. Whatever form they may come in, these souls are your happy place, your comfort, your sunshine, your *everything*, and you genuinely could not imagine life without them in it.

SOFT HEARTS

Never underestimate the quiet ones with the gentle hearts. They will put their heart on the line for the chance to hold yours and will love you selflessly and more softly than you have ever been loved before.

STAY OR GO

This is for anybody who is overthinking a situation that you know you have grown out of. Please don't remain in a situation that isn't fulfilling your soul purely because of the time you have already invested. Yes, you may have invested a lot but you still have the same amount of years left on this earth whether you stay or go, and the quality of those years is dependent on your decision. Wouldn't you rather spend the years you have left with someone who makes life better each day, rather than with someone who constantly makes you feel like you deserve more out of this life?

OVERSTAY

I really do think it's beautiful
the way your heart wants to stay
even when it's been broken
but I really wish
you could see how much
more you deserve than that.

BARE MINIMUM

Please don't stay with someone
who does not respect you.
When it comes to romantic love,
respect is not earned,
It is the bare minimum.

HINDSIGHT

Don't be hard on yourself for not knowing better when you needed to. Some lessons are only learned by going through the difficult times and getting to the other side. That's growth and you should be immensely proud of yourself for reaching the other side.

HAPPINESS IN MY HANDS

Happiness just feels different when you find it within your-self instead of within another person. It feels like *forever* when you know it can't be taken away from you at the hands of others.

I
Just
Want
You
To
Fall
More
In
Love
With
Yourself
And
Your
Life
With
Each
Day.

Keep going.
Don't get so scared
that you crawl back
into that life
you said you don't
want to live anymore.

YOUR TURN

Your turn is coming, your time is coming, your happiness is coming. Even if it feels like you have been celebrating the happiness and success of others a lot lately, make sure you don't forget about all the things you already have to be grateful for. You may not have it *all* just yet, but you are a work in progress, and there is still so much falling into place for you. Your journey may look a little different but I promise you it isn't any less worthy of recognition. There are moments so worth celebrating that are unfairly overlooked. So instead of feeling like you can only smile for other people, normalize feeling proud of yourself for ending a toxic relationship instead of staying with them for the sake of being in a relationship, normalize being proud of yourself for leaving a job where you had the opportunity to progress your career but it was destroying your soul in the process, normalize being proud of yourself for putting your life on hold as you heal. It gets exhausting saving all your smiles for other people so please don't forget how far you have come and how proud of yourself you should be. Don't let your impatience cause you to grow cynical. Everything coming to you is worth waiting for, just don't forget to celebrate everything along the way.

Never let go of your boundaries.

Let go of the people that
question them.

AS YOU ARE

You are doing enough.
You have achieved enough.
You are successful enough.
You are worthy enough.

Don't let the things you're working on
distract you from the things you already are.
Because no matter where you are right now,
you are enough just as you are.

It's okay if
the only person
you're saying
'I love you' to today
is yourself.

ENOUGH SPACE

Let go of competitive energy.
There is enough space for everyone
to be all that they dream to be.
Including you.

This is your reminder that
you should never feel the need
to constantly prove your worth
to the people who have genuine love for you.

Stop seeking validation
from the people who make you
question yourself in the first place.

TIMELY BEGINNINGS

You do not need to wait for a new year, a new month, a new week or a new day to start over. You can decide right now if you want better, and start again at this very moment. Sometimes the perfect time to begin again is right now.

Sometimes you need to let go
of the people you love
because they do not want
the same things as you.

Sometimes you need to let go
of one version of your future
to give yourself the future
you have always imagined.

Sometimes the people you choose
are not meant for you
not because you don't adore them
but because your paths don't align.

As hard as it is
don't give up who you are
or what you always wanted
to make it work for someone else.

HOLD

If your heart is capable
of loving the ones
who did not treat you right,
your heart is capable
of holding yourself
just a little bit more tight.

The world can wait.
You should never feel guilty
about taking a break
and prioritizing your mental health.

CHASING HAPPINESS

Too often we chase this idea of '*happiness*' without even knowing what happiness means to us or what we need to do *(or stop doing)* in order to find it. The thing we sometimes forget is that happiness means different things to different people, and that each of us need to put in the work to learn how it will manifest within us.

The pressure you put on yourself
is not necessary for your growth.

AN INEVITABLE ENDING

On the days that you are missing them, and your heart is hurting over the fact that they ended it, remind yourself to be grateful that you're not spending your *whole* life with someone who has already let you go. Imagine how much happier you will feel knowing that the person beside you is grateful to be there, instead of waking up each day with someone who wishes they were elsewhere. Even on the days that you miss them, trust that it ended exactly when it needed to.

—*It may have ended, but it had to.*

READJUSTING

The difficult part of growing is losing and finding yourself over and over again. Our sense of identity is one of the strongest connections we have with ourselves and when we lose it, it feels like we are losing touch with reality and the world around us. When you think about it, we are made up of little fragments of everything we have been through, everyone we have met, how we have been raised, how we have been treated by others and how we treat ourselves. Remind yourself that it's normal to feel like you are losing yourself when things are changing in your life. You just need some time to readjust and you will come back home to yourself once you have learned what you need to learn in this phase of your journey.

RELEARNING LOVE

If the way you were loved in the past made you feel like you had to be perfect to feel worthy, that you needed to put others first to be lovable, or you needed to overachieve to be seen…I want you to know that you do not have to love yourself in the way that you've been *'loved'* in the past. You are capable of showing yourself love and compassion even if you didn't feel it from the ones you craved it from the most. Remember to soothe your wounds and give yourself all the love that you've always needed.

THIS MOMENT

This is your reminder to be present. Stop living your life in a day, week, month, or year that hasn't yet begun. Life moves far too quickly to be living in a time other than this moment. If you spend too much time worrying about the future (or the past) you'll miss all the beauty around you right now.

Keep going.

Keep growing.

CHARLOTTE FREEMAN is an author from Queensland, Australia, who writes pieces that resonate, from one soul to another.